Dolphin

Monkey

Bee

Hedgehog

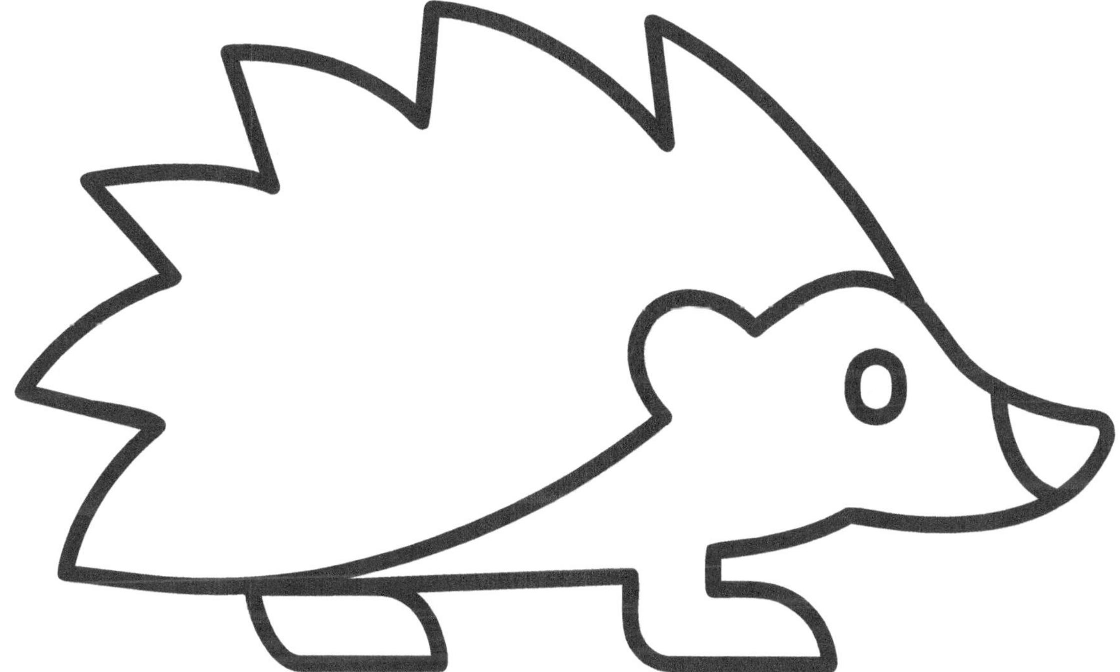

Bear

Penguin

Elephant

Shark

Snake

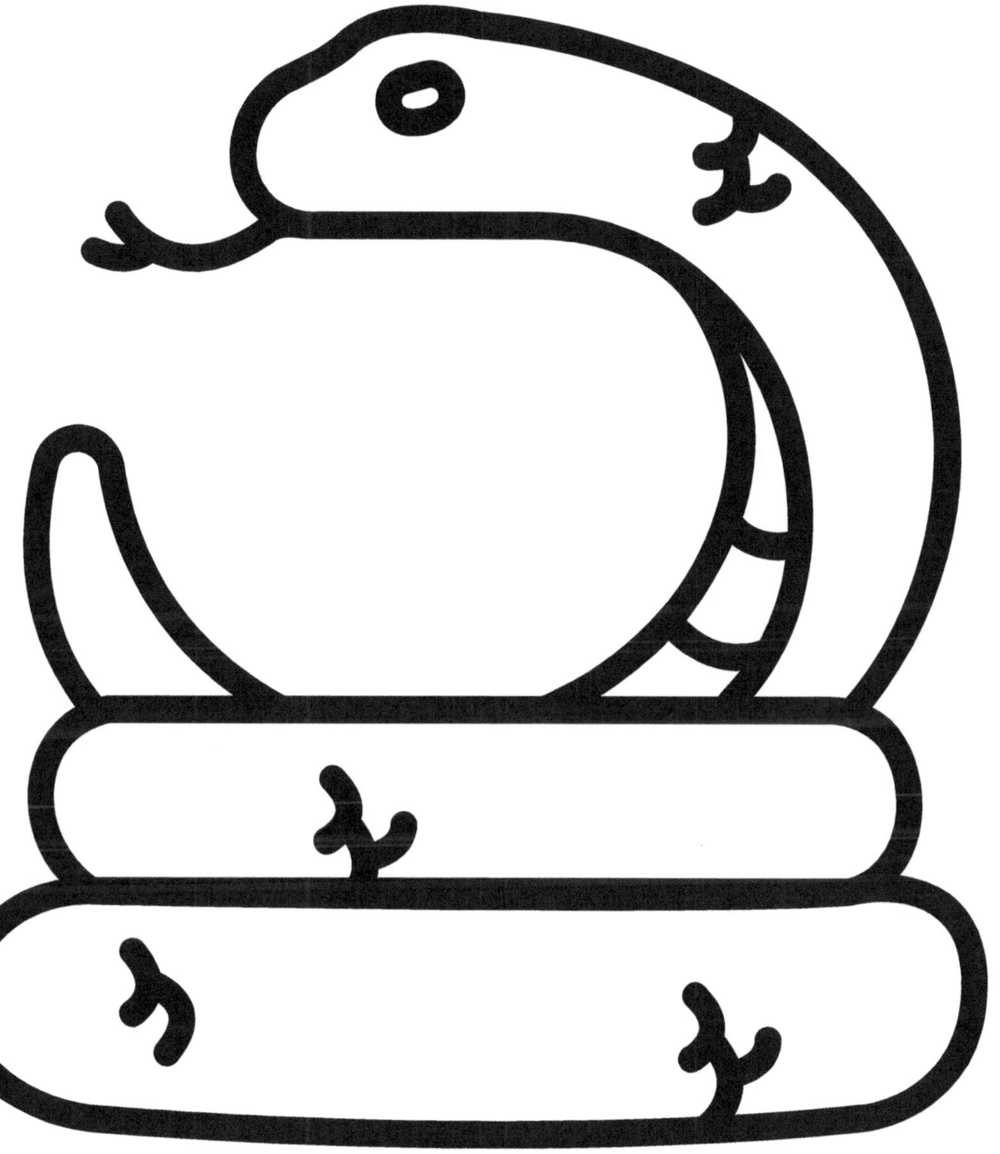

Hummingbird

Eagle

Ladybug

Moth

Butterfly

Bee

Bat

Ant

Scorpion

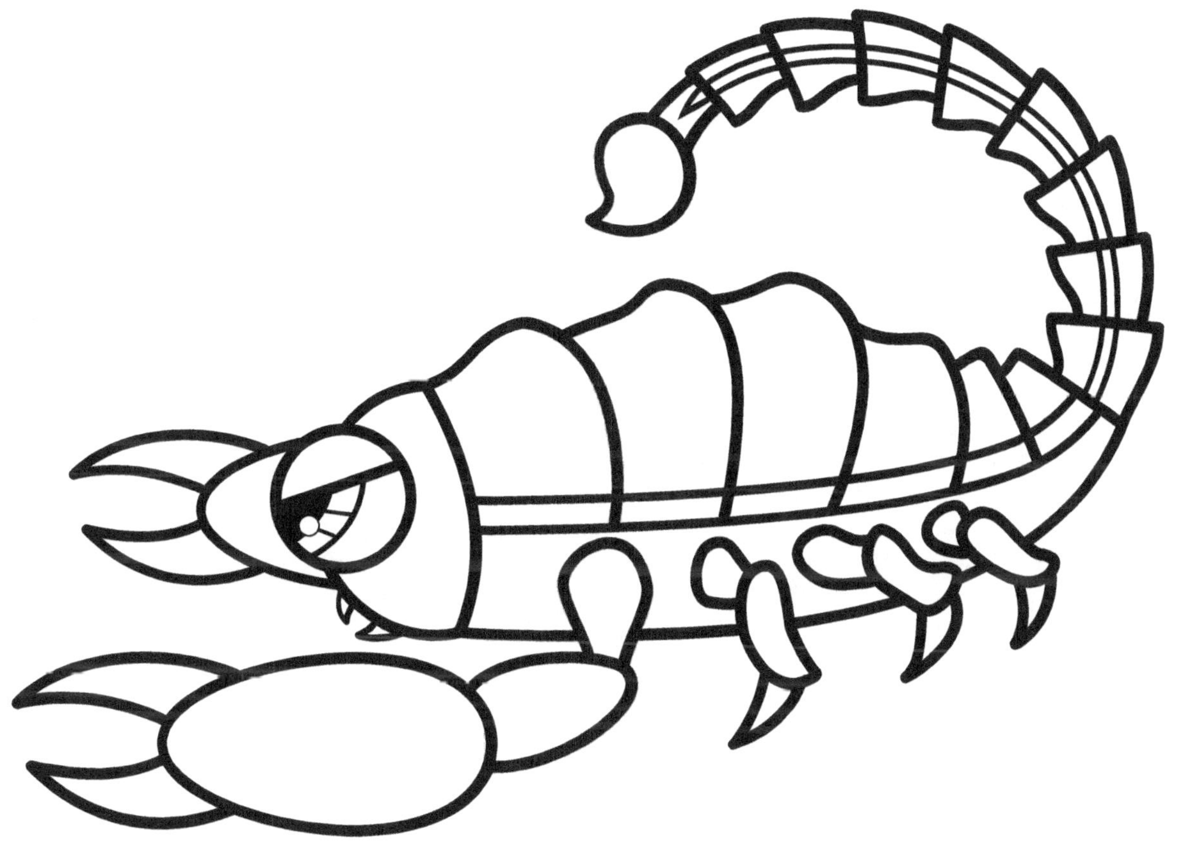

Crab

Bird

Frog

Owl

Porcupine

Pelican

Cheetah

Llama

Koala

Gecko

Bison

Pig

Rhino

Fish

Crocodile

Iguana

Donkey

Salamander

Turtle

Fox

Reindeer

Peacock

Gorilla

Monkey

Bull

Moose

Warthog

Mouse

Chipmunk

Platypus

Kangaroo

Zebra

Lion

Cat

Flamingo